ARMOR OF GOD

WARFARE BY DUCT TAPE

DISCLAIMER AND TERMS OF USE AGREEMENT

ISBN-13: 978-1-942006-02-2

TABLE OF CONTENTS

THE WORD~EPHESIANS 6:10-18

THE ARMOR 4

ARMOR INSTRUCTIONS 5

EPHESIANS 6:10-18

Finally, my brethren, be **Strong** in the Lord, and in the **power of his might.** Put on the whole Armor of God, That ye may be able to Stand against the wiles of the devil. FOR WE WRESTLE NOT AGAINST FLESH AND BLOOD, but against principalities, against powers, against the rulers of the darkness of this world, AGAINST SPIRITUAL WICKEDNESS IN HIGH PLACES. Wherefore take unto you the whole armour of God, that ye may be able to withstand in the evil day, and having done all, to stand. Stand therefore, having your loins girt about with Truth, and having on the breastplate of Righteousness, And your feet shod with the preparation of the gospel of Peace; Above all, taking the shield of Faith, wherewith ye shall be able to quench all of the fiery darts of the wicked. And take the helmet of Salvation, And the Sword of the Spirit, WHICH IS THE Word of God. Praying always with all prayer and supplication, watching thereunto with all perseverance and supplication for all saints.

THE ARMOR

BELT~ CINGULUM MILITARE

The Romans wore a belt made with leather and metal strips that only covered the front of the body. The strips usually went from the waist down to a couple inches above the knee. They didn't usually wear armor on the legs. Metal circles with a boss in the center clacked together when the soldier moved. A boss is a metal point that sticks out, usually on the front of a shield and is part of the handle. The side benefit of the belt was that it made a jangling noise when the Romans marched and it was said to have intimidated the enemy.

BREASTPLATE~LORICA SEGMENTATA

The breastplate armor used during the Roman times was built out of strips of iron and tied together with strips of leather. The strips were arranged horizontally, overlapping downwards and protected the body on both sides. This piece of armor protected the upper body from blows and stabs of the enemy. The breastplate was used during the height of the Roman Empire. It was the standard equipment for the soldiers of that period.

SHOES~ CALIGAE

Our shoe design is actually not an accurate replica of the Roman equipment. They normally wore what looked like sandals but were actually Roman military boots. Caligae were constructed from three leather layers of which the top formed the outer shell. They were laced up the center of the foot and onto the top of the ankle. Iron studs were hammered into the soles, to provide the caligae with protection to their feet, traction and another weapon, allowing soldiers to cause damage by stomping.

SHIELD~SCUTUM

The Roman shield, or Scutum, was made of wood covered with painted leather and had an iron boss in the center, which was part of the handle. It was rather large, large enough to protect most of a legionary, rectangular shaped with a slight outward-facing convex curve. In reality, the shield could repel fiery darts. The shield was one of the most vital pieces of equipment a Roman soldier would have.

SWORD ~GLADIUS

The Romans typically used a short sword instead of a longer sword. The Romans originally learned about the short sword while fighting Iberian mercenaries in the first Punic war. They saw its deadly effectiveness in close quarters. They made it the standard hand-to-hand weapon soon after. It's good for fighting in close quarters and when there are people standing behind you – it does not take much room to swing. It was a short, about fifteen inches long, double-edged iron (and later steel) sword. The sword was so strong it could pierce through wooden shields and armor.

HELMET~ GALEA

The helmet design is based off of the Roman Coolus type from the first century A. D. It was made of bronze and later iron. The Roman officer or centurion would often have a crest on top of his helmet, while the common soldier did not. The obvious purpose of the helmet was to protect the head and face while deflecting the blows of the enemy.

ARMOR INSTRUCTIONS

Ephesians was a city that would have had Roman soldiers. Their armor would have been very familiar to the Christians in Ephesus. When Paul described the pieces of the armor he was using a picture that the Christians could easily understand.

INTRODUCTION:

PVC pipe tips: You can find PVC pipe at your local hardware store like Lowe's and Home Depot. You will need a saw to cut the PVC pipe to the correct length. If you do not have a saw, the large hardware stores will usually cut it for you.

PVC pipe insulation~the black foam stuff. We usually buy this at the same stores as the PVC pipe. We like the kind that comes in a 4 pack of 3 foot pieces.

Cardboard: It can be difficult to cut cardboard so younger children might need some help or supervision. In most of the pieces that use cardboard, it is important to cut the cardboard so the "ridges" (inner corrugated sections) **run across** the narrow width of the piece. This way the piece can bend properly. Check instructions before tracing the pattern onto the cardboard.

½ Width Piece of Duct Tape: Before we begin the weapon instructions, we need to define a term we will use in the book: "½ width". To make a ½ width piece of duct tape, take a piece of duct tape and tear it lengthwise (the long way). Now you have two ½ width pieces of duct tape. Sometimes, even a ¼ width piece of duct tape is used. Just tear the ½ width piece again to make the ¼ width.

Now on to the fun!

BELT OF TRUTH~

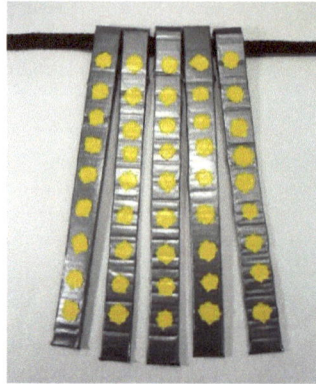

Materials:

Cardboard (see instructions)

Duct Tape

Scissors

Ruler

Your own belt, piece of rope or creation of your choice

Directions:

There are 5 strips. You can make more if you like. The Romans wore a belt with leather and metal strips that only covered the front of the body. The strips usually went from the waist down to a couple inches above the knee.

Please see the note in the introduction about cutting the cardboard. Make sure the "ridges" go across the strip.

For each strip, you need one piece of cardboard. The width is about 1 ½ inches. Measure the length from the waist to slightly above the knee (or wherever you want it) and add 3 inches. So, measurement + 3 inches=length. The 3 inches will fold over your belt. If your belt is wide, add a little more to the length of the cardboard strip. Cut 5 strips.

In our example, the cardboard strip is 1 ½ inches wide by 22 inches long.

Cover the whole piece of cardboard with duct tape. Take a piece of duct tape about 6 inches longer than the strip. Lay the duct tape sticky side up and center the cardboard strip on it. Fold over the ends and press up the sides. Do again covering the other side of the strip.

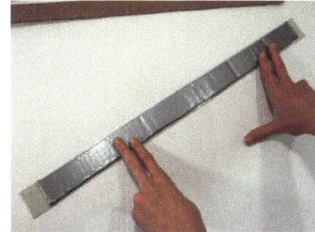

Do this for all 5 strips of cardboard.

Bend over one end of the strip about 3 inches. Test to make your belt will go through the opening. Tape it down firmly.

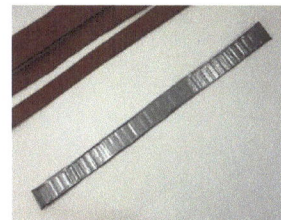

Decorate with "circles". In order to make a "circle" out of duct tape, use two small squares of the same size and place the second square at an angle over the first square. It will give an appearance of a circle. (This is duct tape, after all! ☺) Place the circles down the strip as shown in the picture. (You might want to make sure all the circles line up on the strips, but is not necessary.)

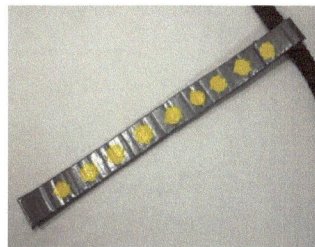

Slide the strips onto the belt and you are done!

You can create your own belt from duct tape and then permanently tape the strips onto it if you like.

BREASTPLATE OF RIGHTEOUSNESS~

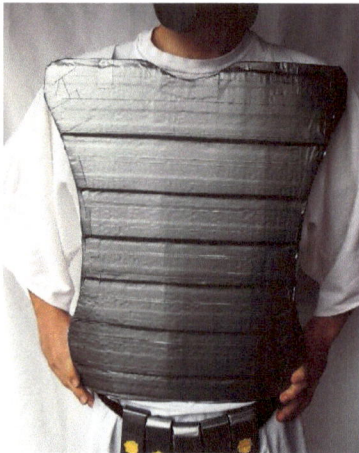

Materials:

Big piece of cardboard (see instructions)

Duct Tape

Ruler/ Marker

Scissors

Elastic or other strap material (see instructions)

Velcro

(You will need a helper on this project.)

Directions:

First, measure for the breastplate. The width is the distance across the shoulders. The length is the distance from the shoulders to the waist. In our example, the cardboard is 19 inches wide and 20 inches long.

Now, to shape the breastplate, hold the cardboard up to the person who will wear it. You are going to have to create your own curves here to fit the person who will be wearing it.

Draw a scooped neckline shape right below the neck. Draw a nice curve on the side so he can reach forward. Round the edges so there aren't any sharp points. Cut out the cardboard on the lines. You can cut one side of the breastplate and use the piece as a pattern for the other side so they are even. ☺

You can try it on the person again to make sure you cut it the way you want it.

If you don't want to do the following option, duct tape the front and the inside of the breastplate and skip to the adding straps step. Otherwise, move on to the stacked strips option.

Option: The Roman breastplate was segmented and had a stacked look to it. For a more authentic Roman look, you can add some strips across the breastplate.

Cut some strips of cardboard about 4 inches wide and a little longer than the width of the breastplate. The size of the breastplate will determine how many you need. We used 6 strips.

Lay the strips onto the breastplate to get an idea of where you want them to go. Remove all but the cardboard strip closest to the bottom (near the waist). Tape this strip onto the breastplate.

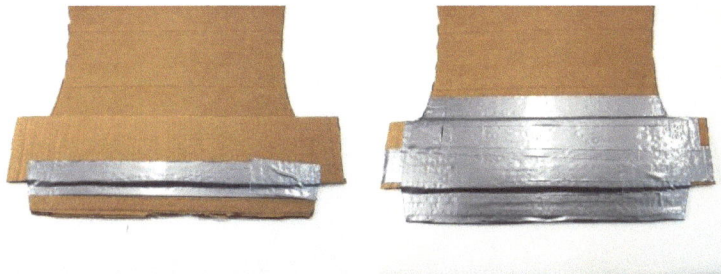

Cover the part below the strip with duct tape.

Turn over the breastplate and trim the cardboard strip so it lines up with the edge of the breastplate. Tape over the edge.

Overlap the next strip and tape it down. Continue working up the breastplate.

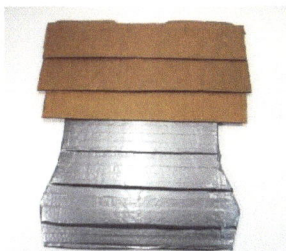

After you get a couple strips taped on, lay out the cardboard pieces you have left to make sure you are spacing them correctly.

Finish adding the strips. Trim all the ends of the strips and cover the edges with duct tape, including the neckline.

Adding the straps:

Hold the breastplate up to the person who will be wearing it and determine where the top ends of the elastic straps will go. The straps should go comfortably over the shoulders (like suspenders). Put a small mark here in the inside of the breastplate.

Estimate the length of the straps by measuring across the back from the mark at the shoulders to the lower inside corner of the breastplate (near the waist). Add a little extra if you are using something for the straps besides elastic. The straps will cross in the back. Cut two (2) straps this length.

Tape the ends of the elastic in place at the shoulders. Staple several times over the end of the elastic and cover the staples with duct tape.

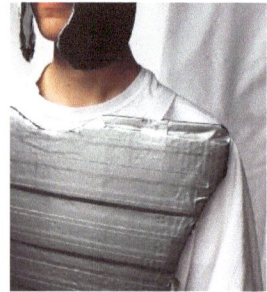

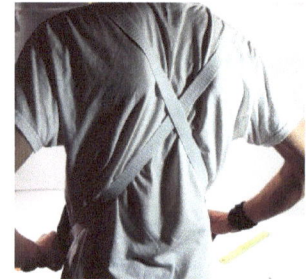

Connecting tabs:

Cut two (2) pieces of elastic 5 inches long. On the bottom, inside corner of the breastplate, tape one piece of the elastic and then staple through the tape and elastic several times. Cover the staples inside and outside with duct tape.

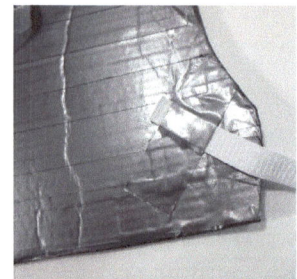

Cut two (2) 2 inch pieces of velcro. Pull the velcro apart. Place the "fuzzy" piece of velcro, fuzzy side up, on the elastic and staple together several times. Cover the back with duct tape to cover the staples.

Do this on both lower corners of the breastplate.

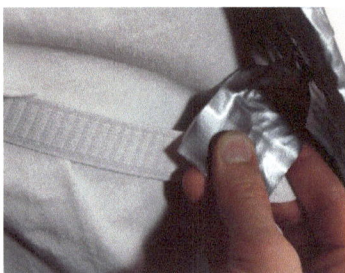

Try on the breastplate again. Cross the elastic straps over the back. Take the loose ends of the elastic straps and line them up with the connecting tabs. Tighten the elastic until is it comfortable. Mark the elastic straps where they meet the velcro. Take off the breastplate.

Place the "pokey" side up of the velcro piece on the elastic strap where you made the mark. Staple several times, firmly. Cover the back with duct tape to cover the staples.

Please note: Always staple onto the velcro so the points of the staples can be covered with duct tape (on the back).

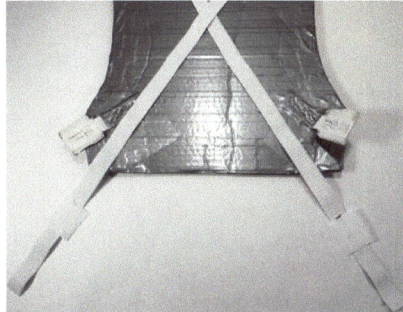

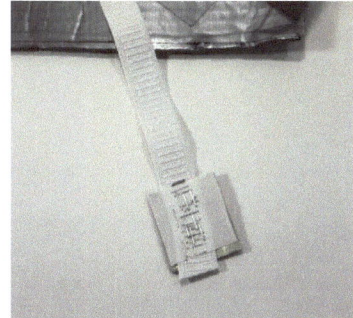

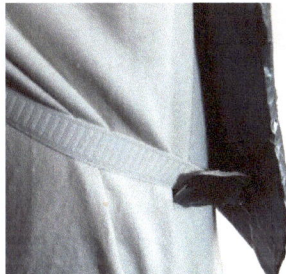

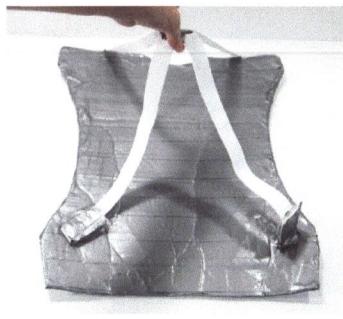

Optional: When the elastic straps are crossed, tape them together at the cross, so the person can get the breastplate on without help. (It is similar to suspenders.)

You could even make the straps from duct tape and put the elastic on the ends of the straps.

SHOES OF PEACE~

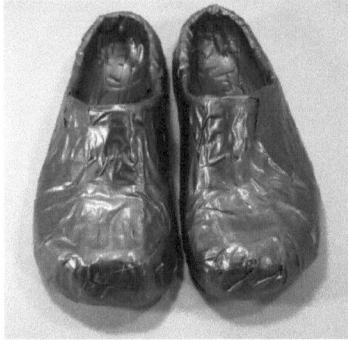

Materials:

Old crocs or sneakers

Duct tape

Directions:

We had hoped to create a more authentic pair of shoes, sandals actually, for this book. But we found it extremely difficult to make with duct tape so we chose to put these armored shoes in the book instead.

Covering old crocs or shoes with duct tape is not very hard. Basically just wrap the duct tape around the shoe neatly without too many wrinkles. If your crocs have holes, we recommend that you put some duct tape on the inside upper part so that the sticky part of the tape won't stick to you!

Please use caution when wearing duct tape covered shoes/ crocs. We found them to be a little slippery on certain flooring. They became less slippery as they were used.

Enjoy!!

SHIELD OF FAITH~

Materials:

Plywood, size and shape of your choice

Four (4) small blocks of wood 3 ½" x 1 ½" x ½"

Cardboard~about 18" x 6"

Duct Tape

Four (4) Screws 1 ½" long (or long enough to go through the blocks of wood, cardboard and plywood)

Saw (to cut plywood if needed)

Screwdriver/ Sandpaper

Scissors/ Ruler   Please Note: This project may require adult help to use the sharp tools.

Directions:

Before you begin cutting the wood, plan the size you want your shield to be. We recommend you measure your arm from the elbow to the knuckles on your hand when you make a fist. The shield should be at least this wide.

Take a piece of plywood and cut to the shape (square, circle, oval, or rectangle) you want for the shield. Either sand the wood or cover the front with duct tape. You may want to add details with duct tape. Usually, we cover the front of the shield with duct tape and sand the back well so that we don't get splinters.

Cut a strip of cardboard 18" long by 4" wide. **: For all cardboard pieces, be sure** to cut the cardboard so the "ridges" (inner corrugated sections) **run across** the narrow width of the piece. This way the piece can bend properly. Cover with duct tape so as to strengthen it. Cut another strip of cardboard 12" long by 2" wide. Also cover with duct tape. Bend up 1 inch on the ends and curve the rest of the piece of cardboard. Do this to both pieces.

The larger piece will go over the forearm. Using your arm, measure where the large piece of cardboard should go on the back of the shield.   (You may need a friend to help you with this.)

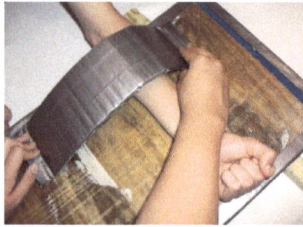

Tape down the ends of the cardboard piece.

Place a block of wood on the end of that piece and screw down on each end of the block. Do this on both ends of the piece.

If you have a power screw driver, you may want to pre-drill the holes. You can use a regular screwdriver also.

Measure where the smaller piece should go by placing your arm in the large piece. You will grip the smaller piece so place accordingly.

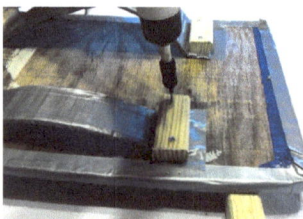

Tape the ends of the cardboard piece to hold it in place. Place a block of wood on the end and screw down on each end of the block. Do this on both ends of the duct tape covered piece.

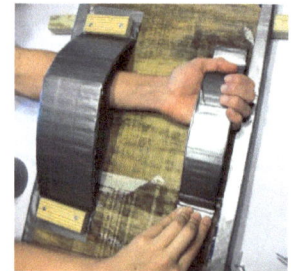

It should look something like this when it is finished.

The shield is done. Good job!! Decorate as you desire.

BUCKLER~

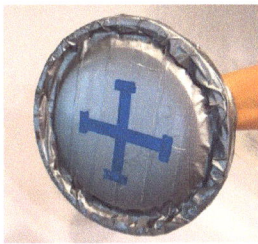

Materials:

Duct tape
Lid from a wheat bucket or ice cream tub
Or a piece of cardboard cut into a circle 13" in diameter or size of your choice

Directions:

Cover the lid with tape. Start with strips across the middle. Cover the entire front. (If using cardboard, cover the back with duct tape, also.)

To make the straps on the back, lay a piece of duct tape sticky side up.

Then cover with a longer strip that goes over the edges. Before you tape the last edge, try it on by laying your arm under the strips. You don't want it too tight. Put 3 more strips over the top of the strap to strengthen it.

Cover the edge with duct tape and decorate as desired.

HELMET OF SALVATION~

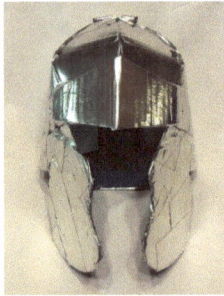

Materials:
Patterns
Duct Tape~Shiny silver looks really nice but it is optional.
Cardstock
Cardboard
Elastic~about ¾" wide by about 8 inches long
Stapler/Staples
Clear "scotch" tape
Scissors
Ruler

Directions:

Print the helmet pieces on cardstock and cut them out. You will need the Roman Upper Helmet, Roman Lower Helmet, Back of Helmet, and Forehead Visor. (If you want the helmet in a smaller size, try minimizing the patterns on a copy machine.)

Tape together the upper helmet pieces at the center front with the "scotch" tape.

Tape together the other edges at the top of the helmet pieces.

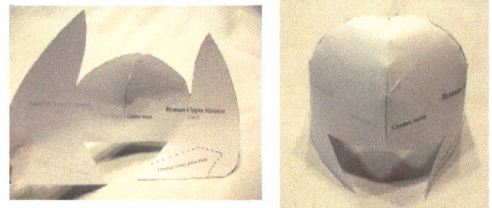

Cut the lower helmet pieces out of cardboard.

Tape lower pieces to upper helmet pieces, matching the overlap dotted lines. Check that the pieces are even with each other.

Cover lower half with duct tape.

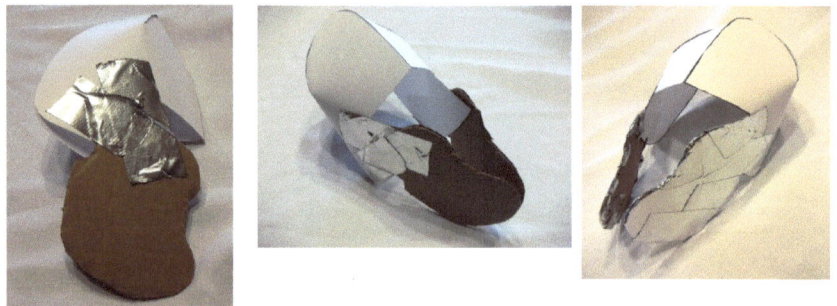

Place a piece of duct tape across the front, right above the eye hole.

Cover the upper helmet with duct tape.

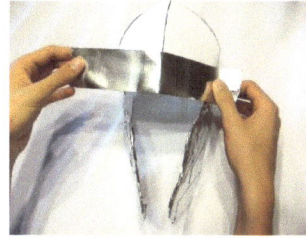

Front forehead piece:

Please note: For all cardboard pieces, be sure to cut the cardboard so the "ridges" (inner corrugated sections) **run across** the narrow width of the piece. This way the piece can bend properly.

Place the forehead visor pattern piece on cardboard, trace and cut out. Bend in half. Cover with duct tape.

Put tape on each small end and tape the forehead piece above eye hole across the brow.

Cover the inside of the helmet with duct tape.

Place the back of helmet pattern piece on cardboard, trace and cut out. (See note on cardboard above.) Bend it to make it curved to fit your head. Cover it completely with duct tape.

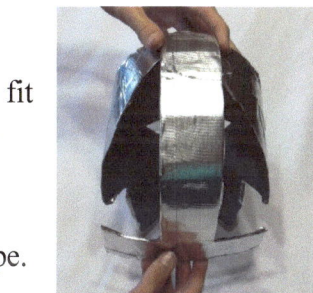

Attach the back helmet piece to the top of the helmet with duct tape. Secure with 2 staples and then cover them with duct tape.

Cut elastic into two (2) 4 inch pieces. Attach elastic to upper helmet by stapling and then covering with duct tape.   **Please note:** Staple away from the inside so the point of the staples are not near the skin.

Tape the other loose end of elastic to the back of the helmet piece. Try on the helmet and adjust fit if necessary. Staple elastic to back of helmet and cover staples with duct tape on both sides.

You're done. Good job!!

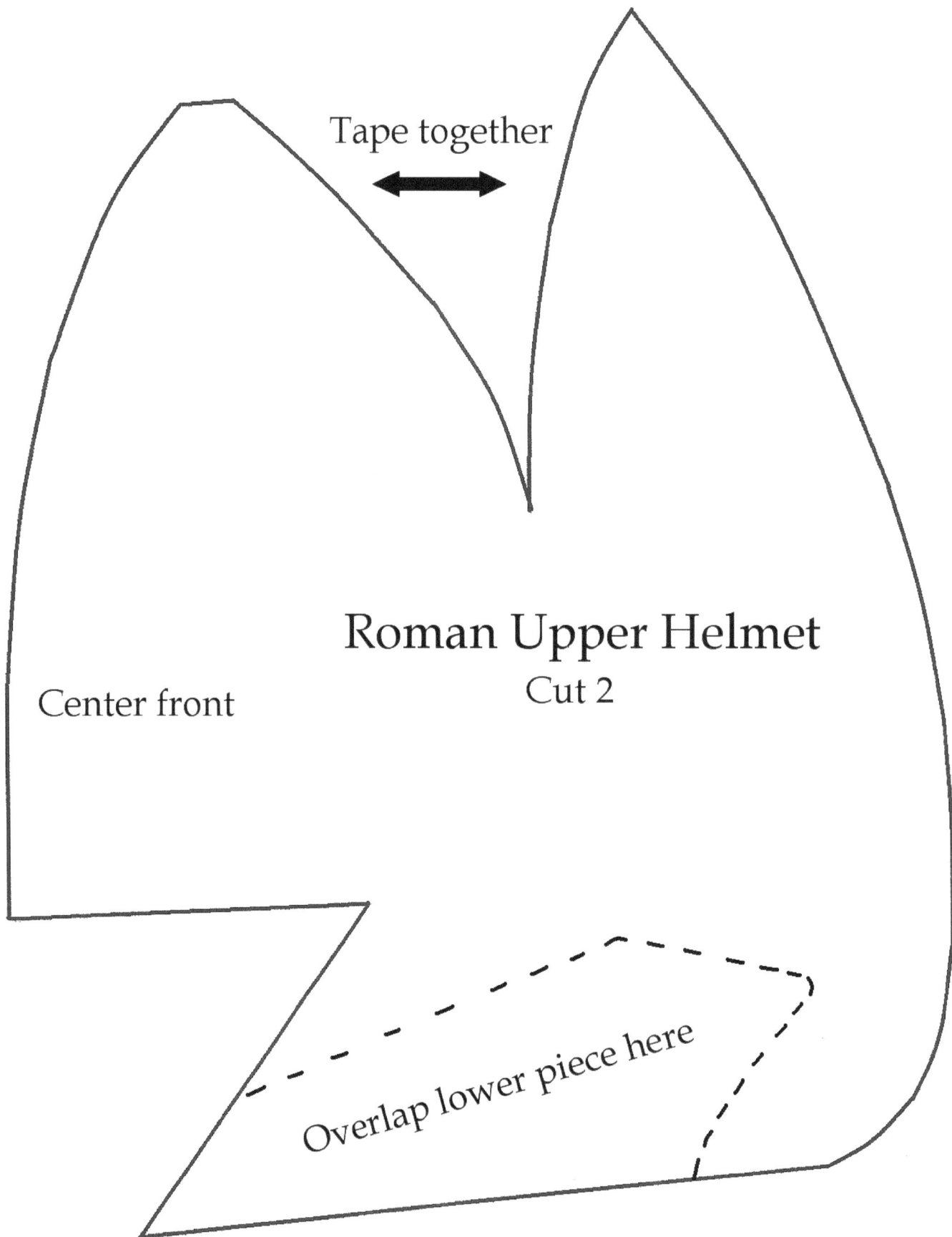

Tape together

Center front

Roman Upper Helmet

Cut 2

Overlap lower piece here

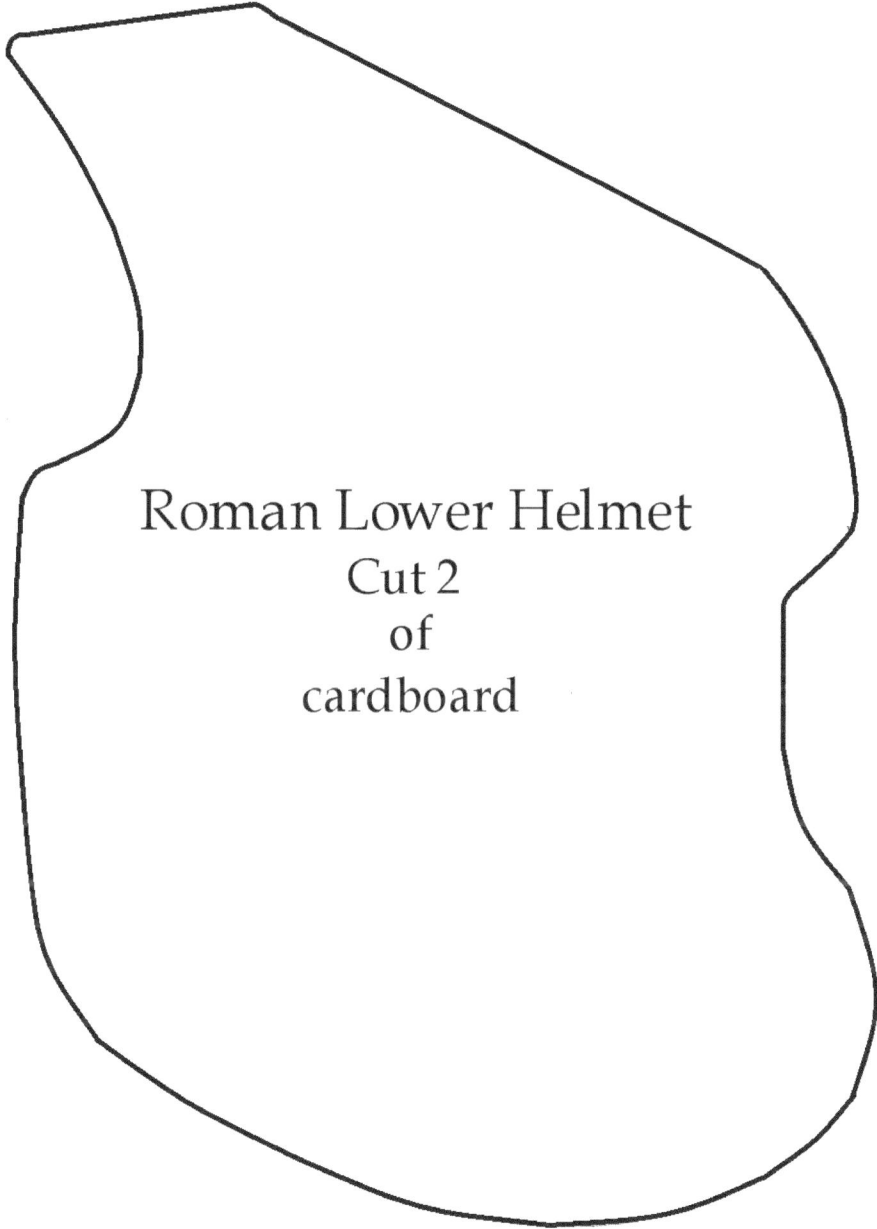

Roman Lower Helmet
Cut 2
of
cardboard

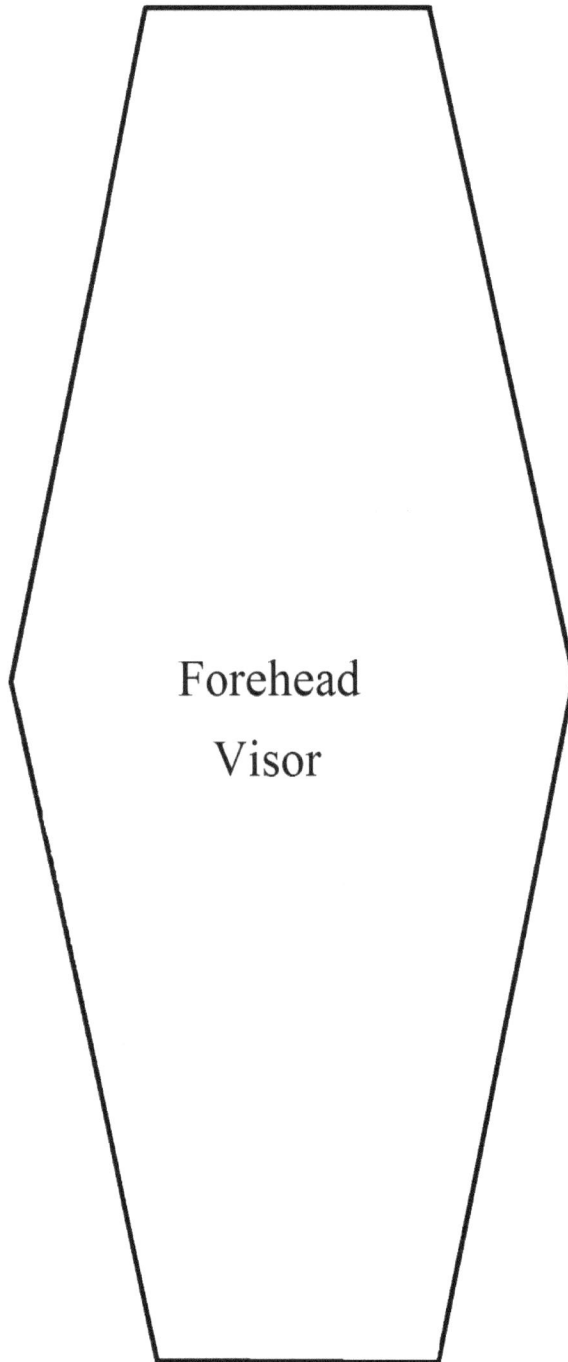

Forehead
Visor

Cut 1
of
cardboard

Back of Helmet

SWORD OF THE SPIRIT~

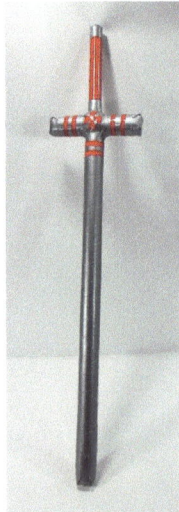

Materials:

3 foot piece of ¾ inch PVC pipe
3 foot piece of PVC pipe insulation
(We use 3/8" thick polyethylene foam, fits ¾" pipe)
Duct tape
Scissors
Ruler
Saw (You may need a saw to cut the PVC to size)

Please Note: This project may require adult help to use the sharp tools.

Directions:

Cut 8 inches off of your 3 foot piece of insulation.

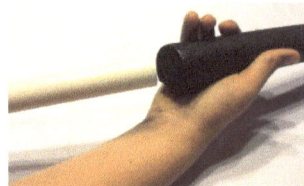

Next, take the larger piece of insulation and slide it down the 3-foot PVC pipe, leaving an inch of insulation past the end of the PVC pipe.

Take the 8 inch piece of insulation foam. Cut a slit 2 inches long in the middle (center) of the piece. On the opposite side, cut another slit.

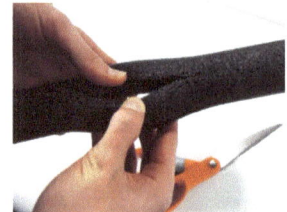

Slide the piece of foam onto the PVC pipe to form the hilt of the sword.

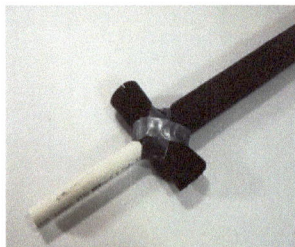

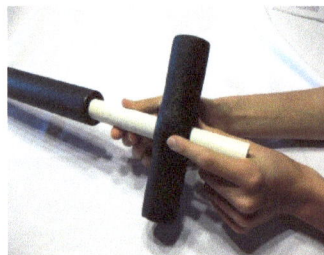

Using a ½ width piece of duct tape, crisscross the duct tape all the way around the hilt to strengthen it.

Tape across the end of the hilt, turn and do it again. Then tape around the end to make it smooth.

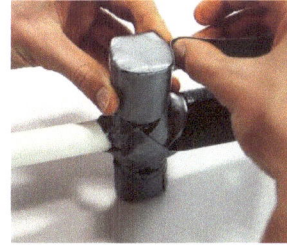

Do this on both ends of the hilt.

Using a ½ width piece of duct tape, tape around the handle and on the blade of sword above and below the hilt.

Tape a piece of duct tape on the very center of the hilt to cover up the black insulation. Cover the entire hilt with duct tape.

Cap the tip of the blade of the sword by taping over the end.
Press down the edges of the duct tape. Turn the sword and tape again. Press down the edges to give a finished look.
Wrap the duct tape around the end a few times to strengthen it so it won't tear during battle.

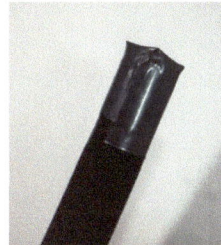

Now tape the blade. It is helpful to have another person. Start at the hilt and wrap on a slightly diagonal angle towards the tip of the blade.

Cap the end just as you did with the end of the blade. Cover the handle with a duct tape color of your choice.

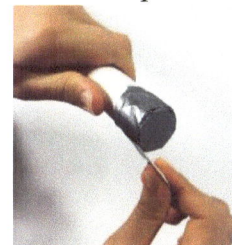

Decorate as desired. Often wealthy Greeks and Romans would put a "jewel" in the center of the hilt.

You're done! Good job!

COSTUMES

TUNIC~

Materials: Some sort of fabric-knit, sheets, cotton or whatever you have
Belt or material for a sash
Ruler
needle and thread

Scissors/
Sewing machine or

Directions:

First determine the size you will need. Most tunics in the Greek and Roman time went down to the knees and had no sleeves. They draped over the shoulders a little bit. The size of your fabric may determine the width or measure across the shoulders. Make it wide enough so that you can slip it over your head and shoulders and get the arms out of the arm holes. If you have enough fabric, double the length so you won't need to sew a seam across the shoulders.

Cut a hole for the head to go through. The No-Sew Option is to just pull the tunic over the head and use a belt to keep it around the waist.

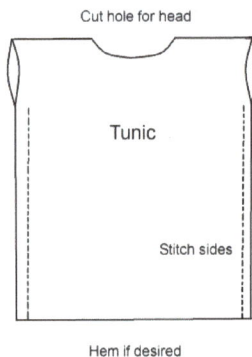

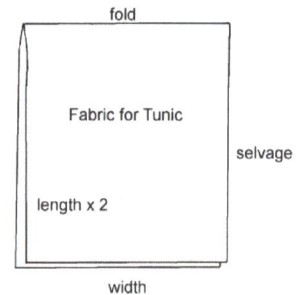

fold

Fabric for Tunic

selvage

length x 2

width

Cut hole for head

Tunic

Stitch sides

Hem if desired

The sewing option is to sew up the sides but leave an arm hole. Hem the bottom if desired. Knit fabric is nice because it doesn't fray and you won't have to hem the edges.

In the early Roman times, soldiers only wore sleeveless tunics. It was considered too feminine to have sleeves. But near the end of the Roman era, it was acceptable to wear sleeves.

If you want sleeves in your tunic, make a "T" shape of fabric and then sew up the sides. Be sure the main body of the tunic is wide enough so that you can get it on and get the arms through the sleeves. Maybe almost double the width across the front of the person.

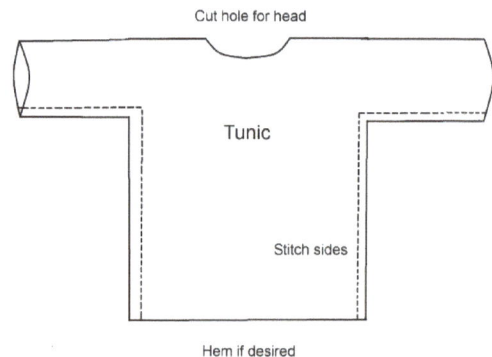

Some children are small and the hole in the neck will gap too much. Just add a button and loop at the back of the neck to close it a little. See Cloak instructions.

Cut hole for head

Tunic

Stitch sides

Hem if desired

Use a belt or cut a strip of fabric to wrap around the waist. The tunic was considered underclothing that was worn under armor or a toga.

CLOAK~

Materials:
Some sort of fabric-knit, sheets, cotton, or whatever you have
Button
Thin piece of elastic, ribbon, or string
Couple of pins
Scissors/ Ruler
Needle and thread

Directions:
Determine the size of cape that you need. Do you want a cloak that goes down to the knees or almost to the floor? That is your length measurement plus an inch to turn over at the neck. The width of your fabric may determine your width of the cloak; otherwise decide how wide you want it.

Cut your fabric to size. If you are using a fabric that will fray, you may want to hem the sides first. Fold over an inch the top edge which will go by the neck. Try it on. Clasp the cape closed a few inches down from the front of the neck. This where you will attach the button and elastic (ribbon). Mark it on both sides with a pin. Sew on the button on one side. Measure a small piece of elastic (ribbon) around the button so you can still get it on and off. Stitch elastic (ribbon) on both ends to the cape at the mark.

Throw over the shoulders and button at the neck.

~BRACAE OR BRACCAE~

The Romans wore pants under their tunics in cooler weather, so if you wear pants under your tunic you will still be authentic.

Warfare by Duct Tape

Visit our website www.warfarebyducttape.com for more information. Also available from Warfare by Duct Tape:

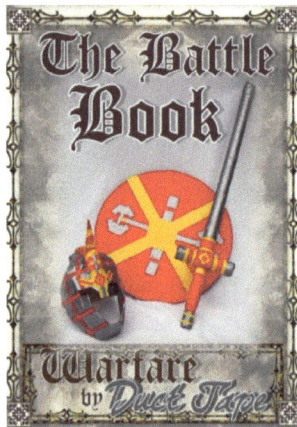

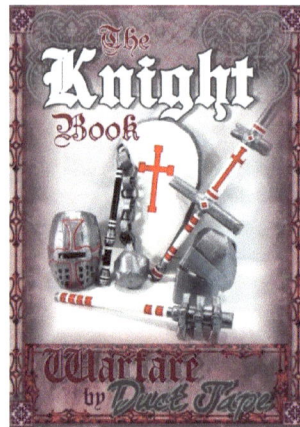

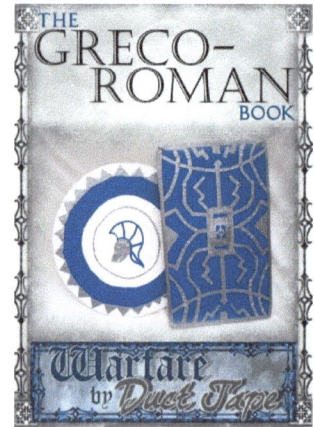

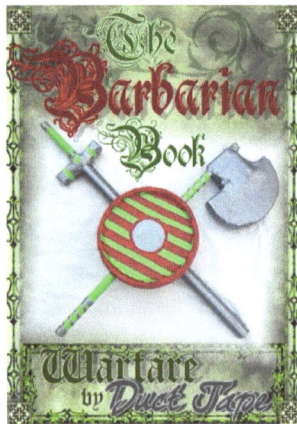

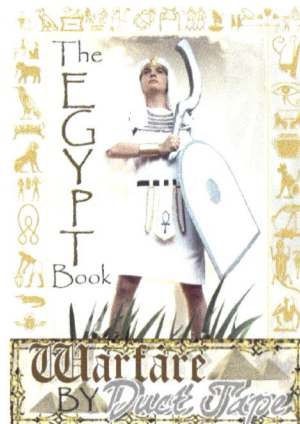

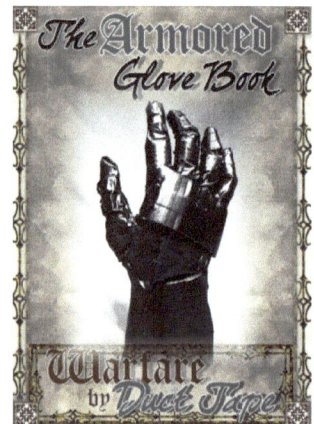

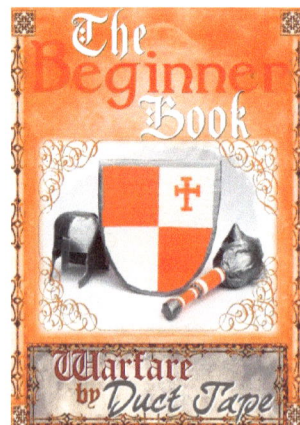

The Battle Book

The Knight Book

THE GRECO-ROMAN BOOK

The Barbarian Book

The EGYPT Book

The Armored Glove Book

The Beginner Book

www.ingramcontent.com/pod-product-compliance
Lightning Source LLC
LaVergne TN
LVHW072123070426
835511LV00002B/74